AF555977

Young Learner's

HOW TO DRAW

Step by Step

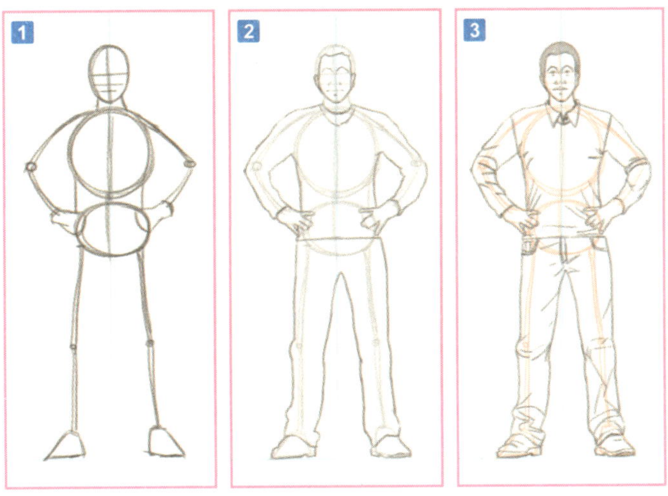

Young Learner Publications®
G-1A Rattan Jyoti, 18 Rajendra Place, New Delhi- 110 008 (INDIA)
Tel: 25750801, 25820556, 25755559 Fax: 91-11-25764396
Website: www.goodwillpublishinghouse.com
E-mail: gph.ylp@goodwillpublishinghouse.com
goodwillpub@gmail.com

Stick Figure Sketches

The first thought that probably crosses every beginner's mind is that, realistic sketches are very difficult to draw. On the contrary, these sketches are very simple to make! In this exercise we shall learn to draw realistic sketches with the help of stick figures. Stick lines represent the spine, the arms and the legs in a simple way. At this stage we shall only capture the posture of the person. We also have to add a basic shape to our stick figure—one oval each for head, chest and hip bone.

Carefully observe and read all the steps to draw the front sketch of a standing man.

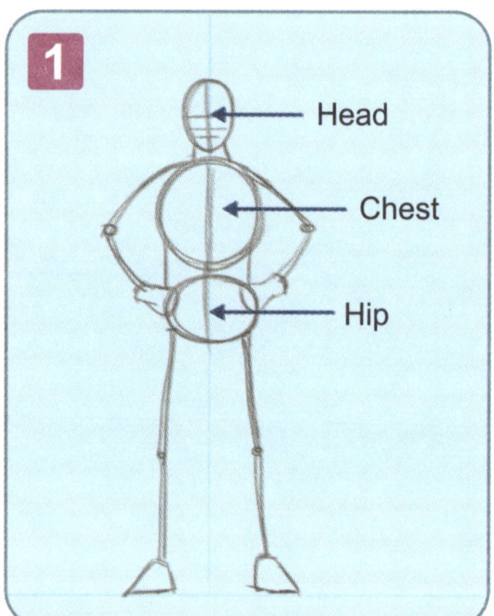

Before we start using stick figures to draw realistic sketches, it is important to practice drawing stick figures. Draw as many different stick figures as you can. Observe people around you like family members, friends, schoolmates, etc. and draw stick figures according to different body shapes and sizes.

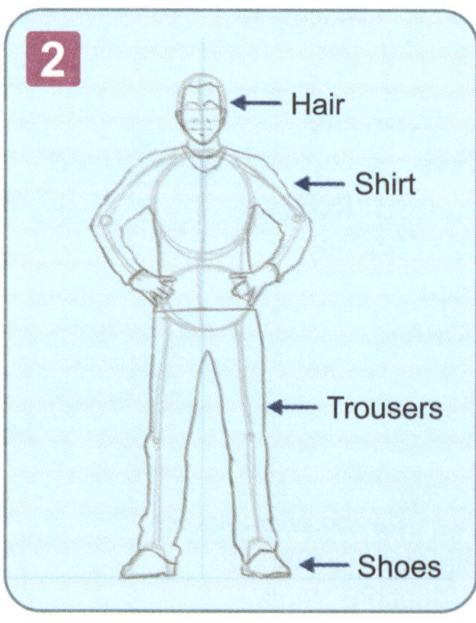

1. Capture the basic posture of the person with stick lines and add basic shapes for head, chest and hip (see figure 1).

2. Draw hair and outlines for hands and clothing like shirt, trousers and shoes (see figure 2).

3. Finally, draw eyebrows, eyes, nose and lips. Also, draw creases for shirt, trousers and details of shoes (see figure 3).

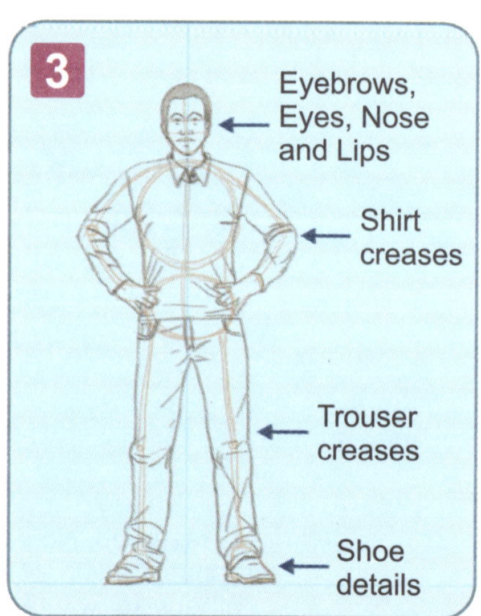

Carefully follow all the steps of drawing the young girl's sketch. Draw using a lead pencil in the boxes given alongside. Remember to draw the stick figures with very light pencil. Once the drawing is complete, darken the final lines and erase the stick figure lines.

1	1	1
2	2	2
3	3	3

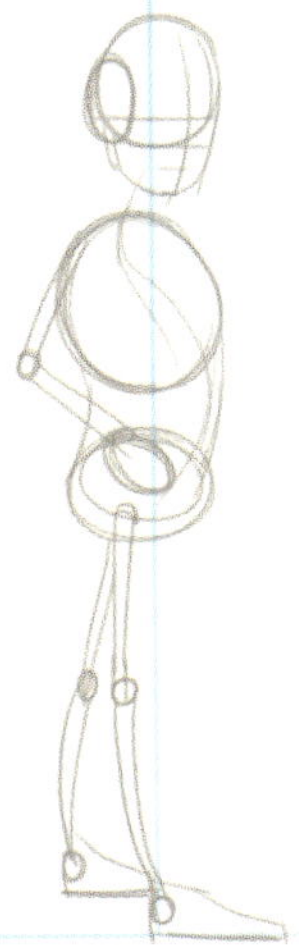

Carefully follow all the steps of drawing the old man's sketch in the sitting position. Draw using a lead pencil in the boxes given alongside. Remember to draw the stick figures with a very light pencil. Once the drawing is complete, darken the final lines and erase the stick figure lines.

1 1 1

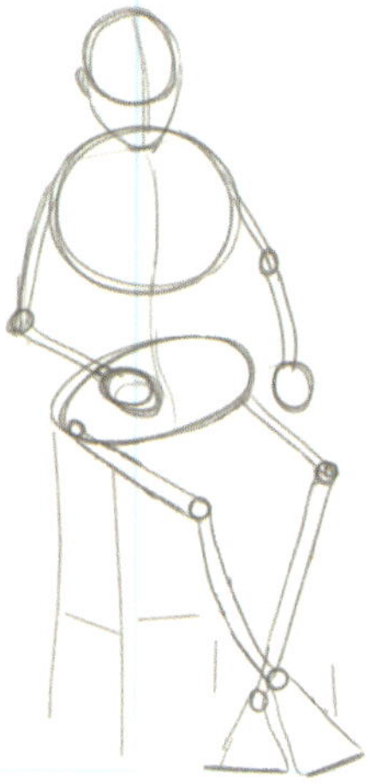

2 2 2

3 3 3

Carefully follow all the steps of drawing the woman's sketch in the standing position. Draw using a lead pencil in the boxes given alongside. Remember to draw the stick figures with a very light pencil. Once the drawing is complete, darken the final lines and erase the stick figure lines.

1 1 1

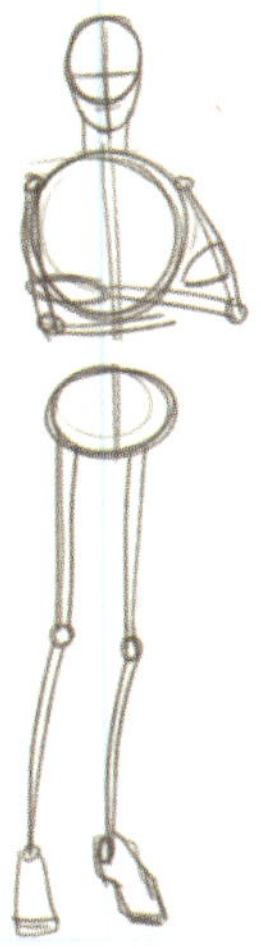

2 2 2

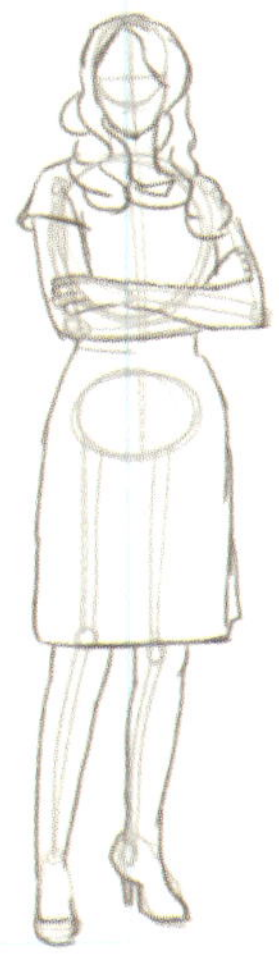

3 3 3

Carefully follow all the steps of drawing the old lady's sketch in the sitting position. Draw using a lead pencil in the boxes given alongside. Remember to draw the stick figures with a very light pencil. Once the drawing is complete, darken the final lines and erase the stick figure lines.

1

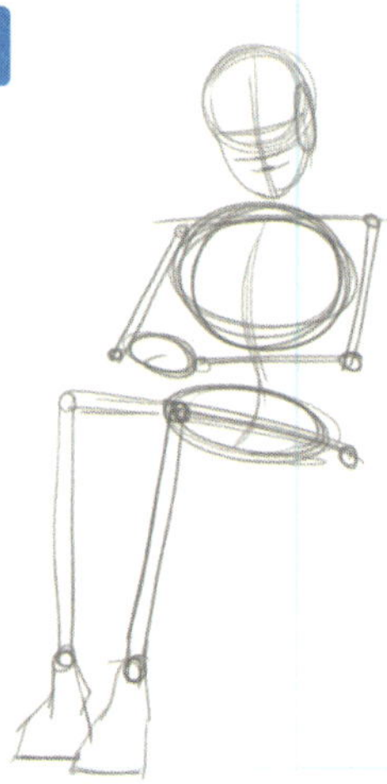

1

1

2

2

2

3

3

3

Carefully follow all the steps of drawing the side pose of the boy in the standing position. Draw using a lead pencil in the boxes given alongside. Remember to draw the stick figures with a very light pencil. Once the drawing is complete, darken the final lines and erase the stick figure lines.

1

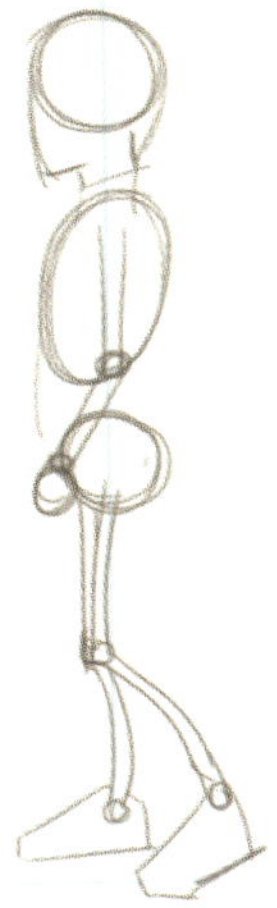

1

1

2

2

2

3

3

3

Composition

In this exercise we shall learn to draw various compositions using different human body sketches. We first need to know what exactly a composition is. A composition is an arrangement of different elements around us. There is no fixed pattern to make a composition. Each composition has an individual quality. But, there are few basic elements of composition in art that are to be borne in mind, namely, **positioning, unity, balance, proportion, overlapping, movement.**

Elements of a composition

1. **Positioning** - Avoid drawing the composition on the final sheet of paper. Start with drawing individual sketches in your sketchbook. Cut out the shapes and then try them out at various positions on the final sheet. Move them around till you get a satisfactory composition. This method is certainly a lot easier and faster than composing directly on the final sheet.

We have used the same method to make the composition given below. We have selected the sketches which we had drawn on previous pages and tried different positions to draw the final composition. You can also try different positions and make a composition by using the same sketches which we have used. If you are making a composition which just doesn't seem right, the first thing you should consider is whether the elements (human figures, objects) in the composition are in the correct position or not.

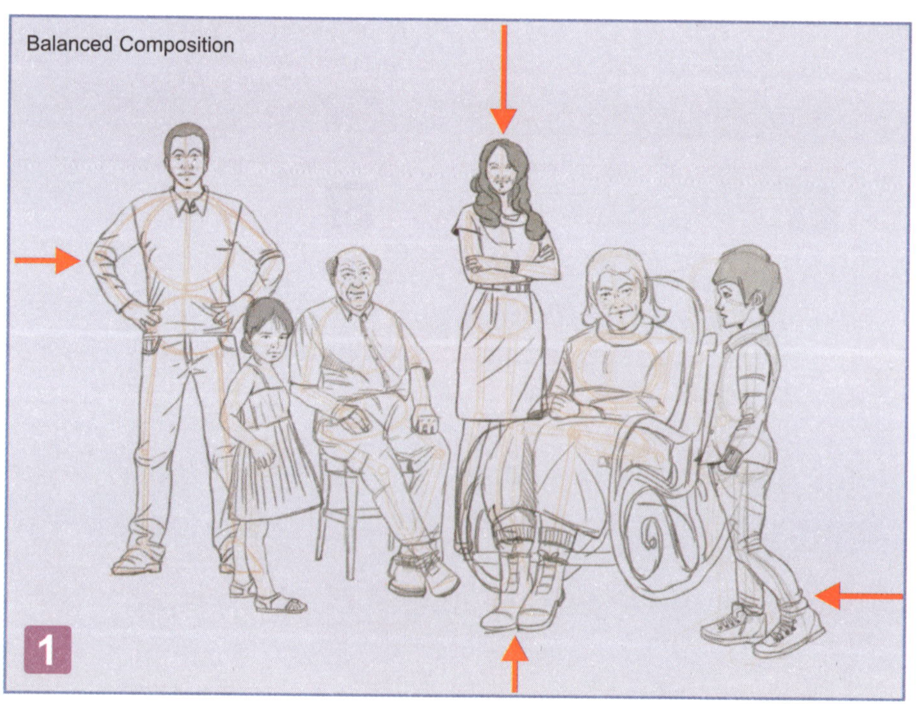

2. **Unity** - The composition is an arrangement of elements of the artwork that unites the elements into one whole. All the elements of composition should blend well and belong together. The textures, patterns and colours also create a sense of balance and unity within the composition.

3. **Balance** - There must be a balance between the sketches and the space around them. Always give more space above head and less space below the feet (see red arrows in figure 1 for guidance).

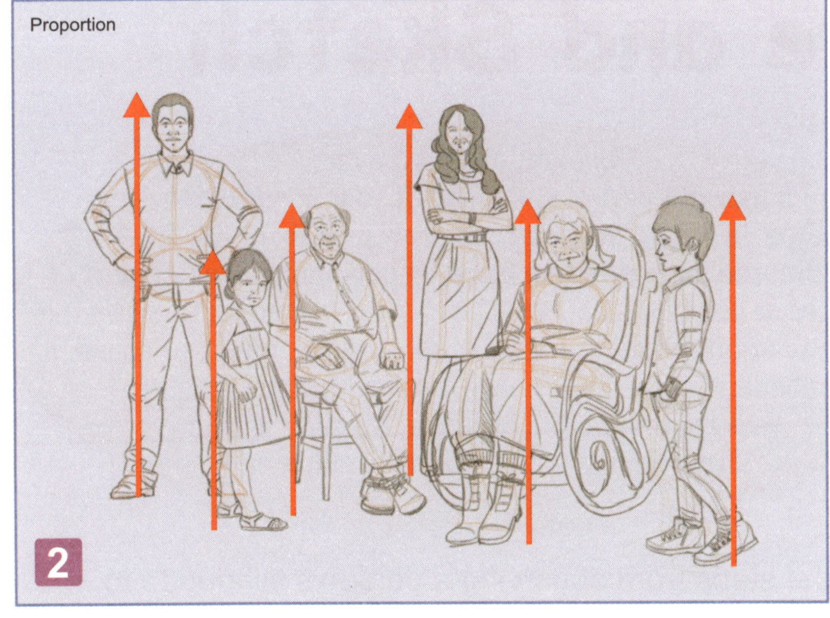

4. **Proportion** - If you observe nature, you will notice that it is very rare that various elements like trees, stones, mountain, etc. lie in a neat line. All these elements exist in different sizes, shapes and colours. This concept of natural variation is applied while creating a composition to make it more interesting. As shown in figure 2, we have first placed a standing man followed by a young girl on the front side. Then, we have placed a sitting old man and a standing woman, both towards the back. We have then placed an old lady in the sitting position and a young boy in the standing position, both in the front.

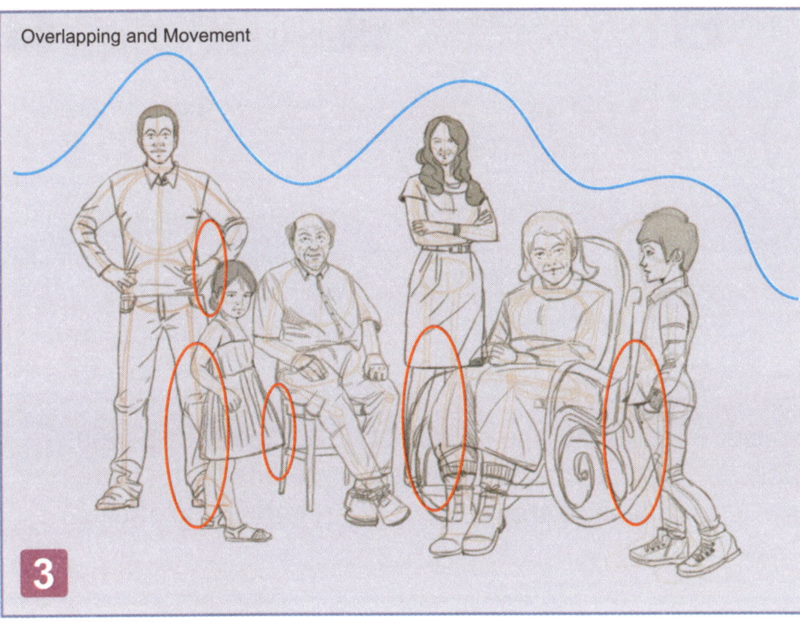

5. **Overlapping** - It is an important part of a good composition to connect the elements of the artwork in one group. In figure 3, the young girl, old lady and the young boy are overlapping other human figures and binding the composition well (shown in red ovals).

6. **Movement** - This is the direction in which the viewer's eyes move through a composition, observing the arrangement of objects and the position of figures (as shown in blue colour in figure 3).

Besides the given composition, it is important to practise drawing different human body posture sketches in your sketchbook. Then, select the sketches from your sketchbook and arrange them in various positions to make different compositions.

Observe and Sketch

Observation is the most important part of sketching. If your observation power is strong then you can draw just about anything easily. But the main problem faced by beginners is which part of the figure or object to observe. The answer is simple! Observe the silhouette or outer shape of the person, animal, object or scene. A silhouette is the dark image outlined against a lighter background. In this exercise, we shall learn to draw figures with the help of silhouette.

Carefully read and understand all the steps from observing a person's silhouette to drawing the final detailed figure.

1. Observe the man's silhouette.

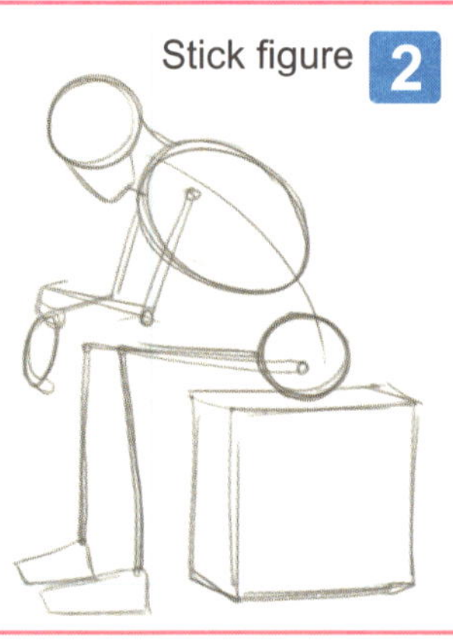

2. Observe the pose and draw its stick figure.

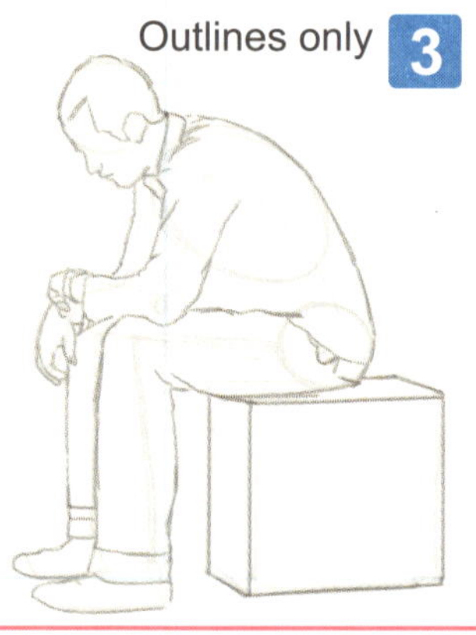

3. Draw the outline of the man's silhouette seen in step 2.

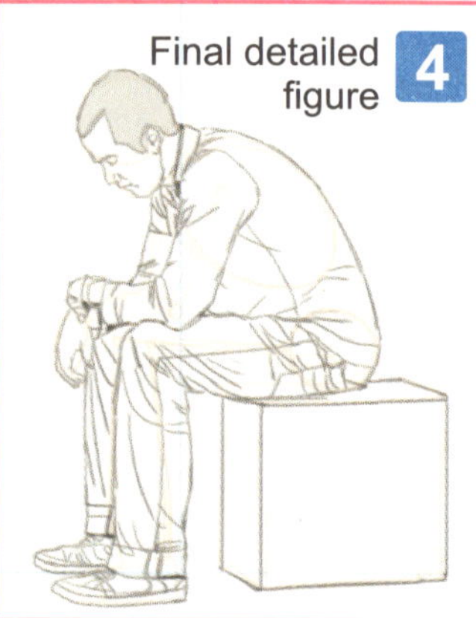

4. Finally draw the details of the body, clothes and shoes.

Carefully observe the man's sitting pose given below. Follow steps 2, 3 and 4, and draw accordingly in the boxes given below. Do not draw the silhouette step (step 1).

Stick figure 

Outlines only 

Final detailed figure 

Observe the girls' silhouettes in the standing pose. Draw the images in the boxes given alongside.

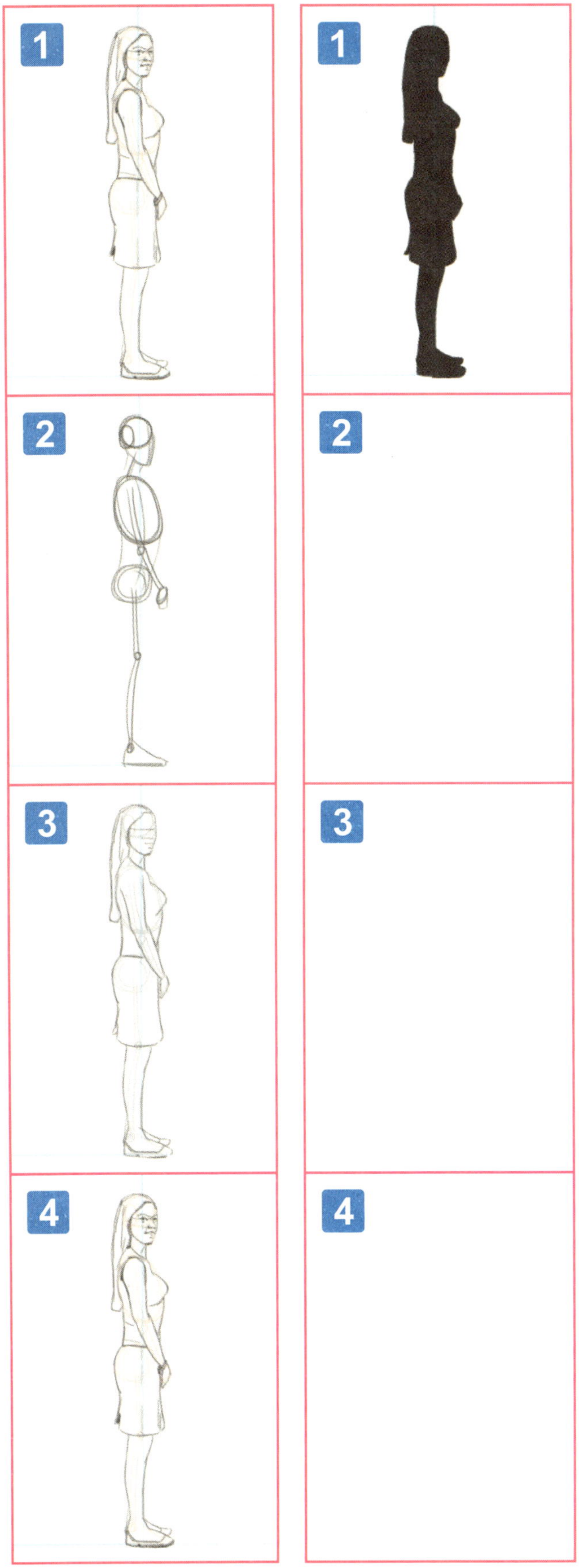

1	1	1	1
2	2	2	2
3	3	3	3
4	4	4	4

Observe the woman's silhouette in a sitting pose. Draw the images in the boxes given below.

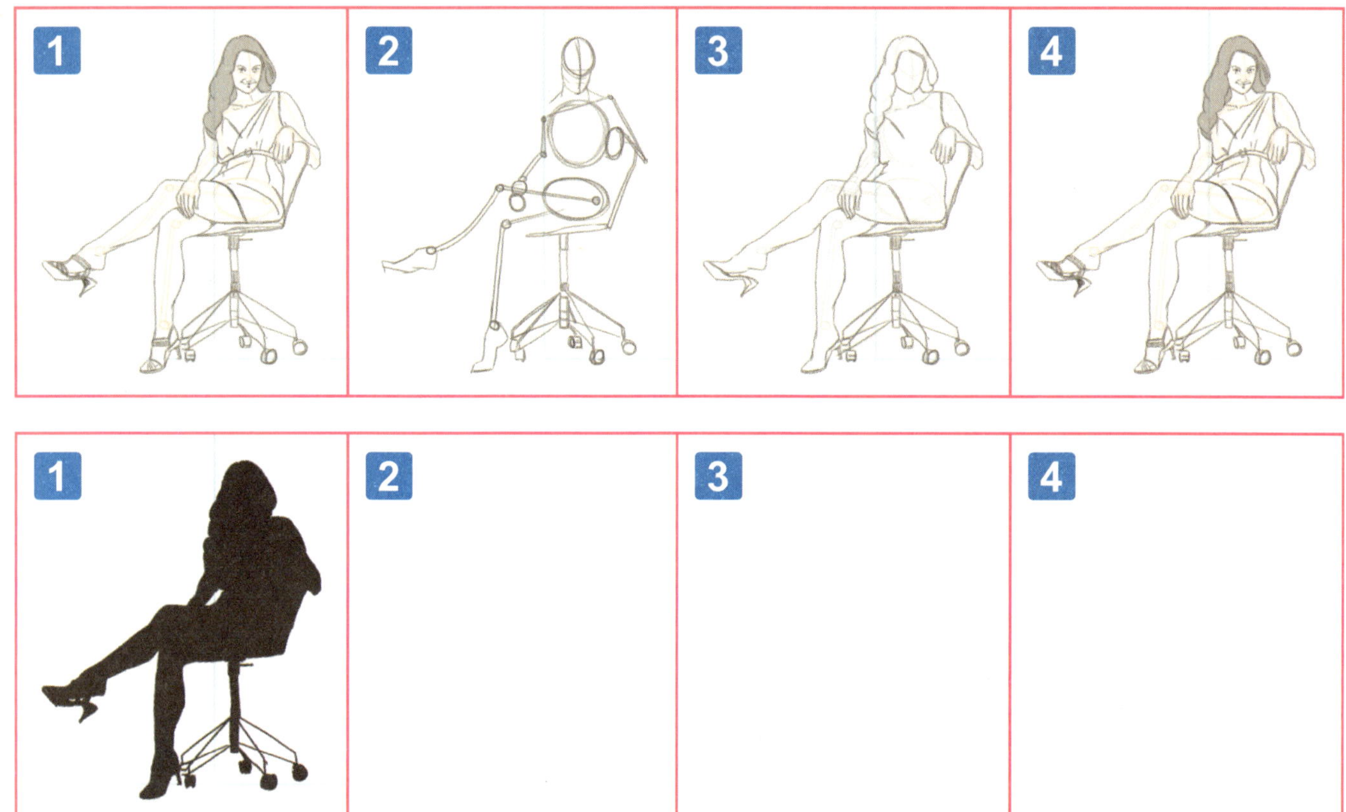

Observe the man's silhouette in a standing pose. Draw the images in the boxes given below.

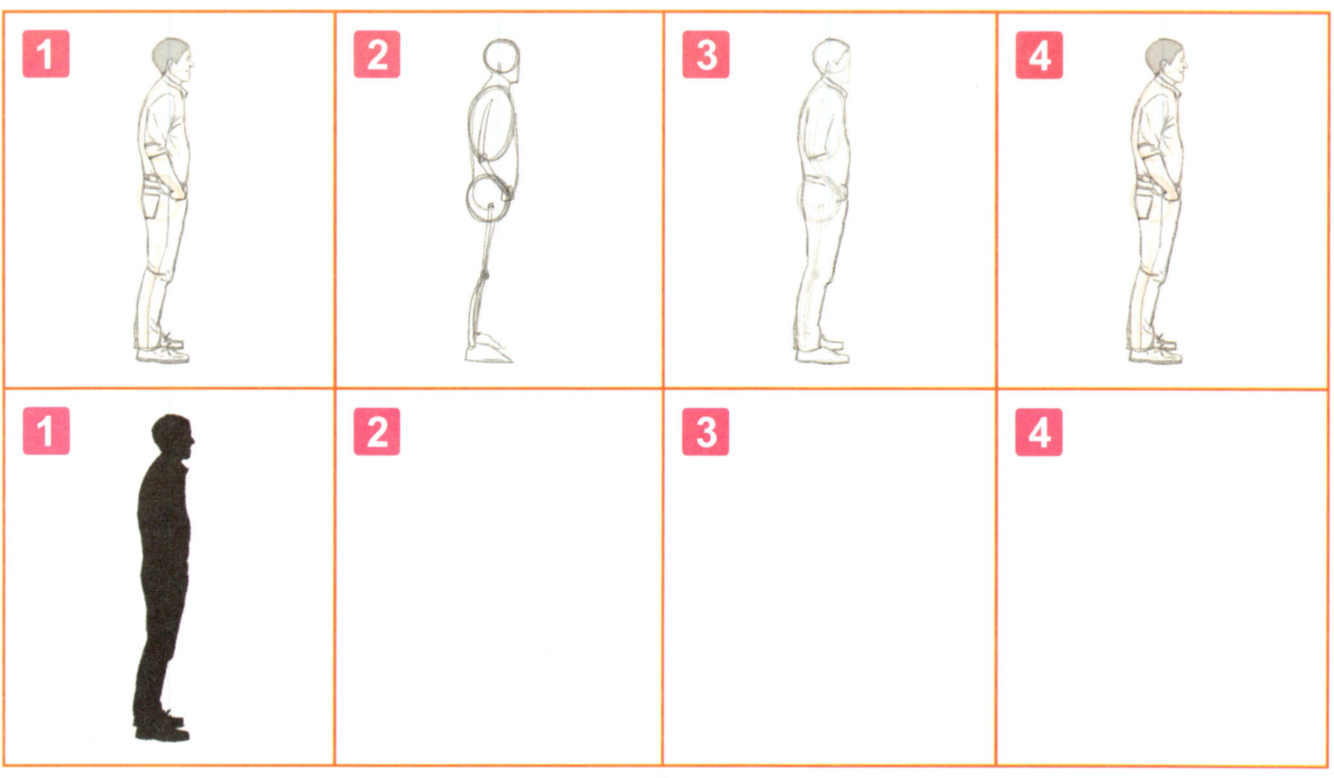

We have selected the sketches which we have drawn on previous pages to make the composition shown below. Follow the steps for the sketches, and draw the same composition using a lead pencil in the box given below. The first step has been done for you.

For teachers and parents: Besides this exercise, encourage the children to practise different compositions in their sketchbooks.

Carefully observe the young boy's standing pose and the young girl's sitting pose silhouettes. Draw them in the boxes given alongside.

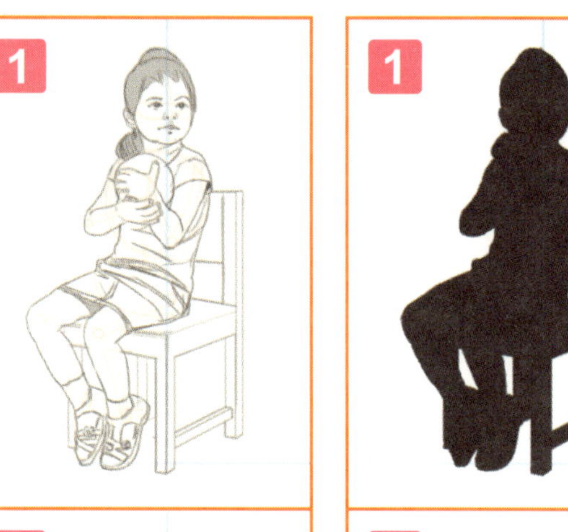

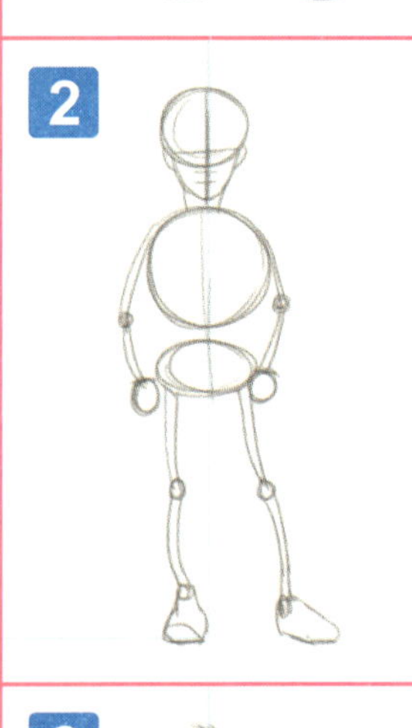

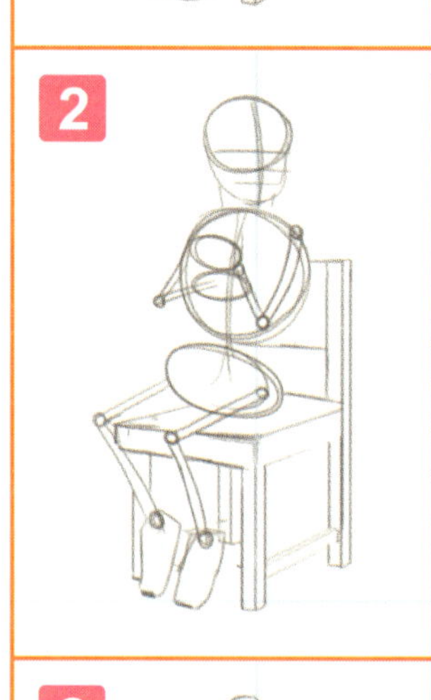

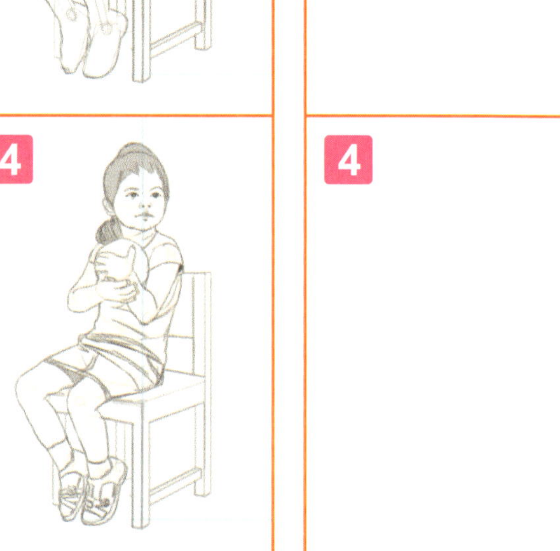

Carefully observe the different poses given below. Visualise their silhouettes. Draw the next three steps for each figure in the boxes given alongside (as shown in previous pages).

We have selected the sketches which we have drawn on previous pages and made the composition shown below. Follow the steps for the sketches and draw the same composition using a lead pencil in the box given below. The first step has been done for you.

For teachers and parents: Encourage the children to practise various compositions of different sports images by using sports magazines as reference.